CINCO DE MAYO

Written by Alice K. Flanagan
Illustrated by Patrick Girouard

Content Adviser: Lydia M. Huante, Education Director, Mexican Fine Arts Museum Center, Chicago, Illinois

Reading Adviser: Dr. Linda D. Labbo, Department of Reading Education, College of Education, The University of Georgia

COMPASS POINT BOOKS

MINNEAPOLIS, MINNESOTA

Compass Point Books
3109 West 50th Street, #115
Minneapolis, MN 55410

Visit Compass Point Books on the Internet at *www.compasspointbooks.com*
or e-mail your request to *custserv@compasspointbooks.com*

Editors: E. Russell Primm, Emily J. Dolbear, and Patricia Stockland
Designer: The Design Lab

Library of Congress Cataloging-in-Publication Data
Flanagan, Alice K.
  Cinco de Mayo / written by Alice K. Flanagan ; illustrated by Patrick Girouard.
    v. cm. – (Holidays and festivals)
Includes bibliographical references and index.
Contents: The first people of Mexico–Living under Spanish rule–The Battle of Puebla–A holiday of freedom!–
Favorite Mexican food–Favorite Mexican music–The Mexican Hat Dance–Celebrating in the United States–
Things you might see on Cinco de Mayo.
  ISBN 0-7565-0480-5 (hardcover : alk. paper)
 1. Cinco de Mayo (Mexican holiday)–Juvenile literature. 2. Mexico–Social life and customs–Juvenile literature.
3. Cinco de Mayo, Battle of, 1862–Juvenile literature. [1. Cinco de Mayo (Mexican holiday) 2. Mexico–Social life
and customs. 3. Holidays.] I. Girouard, Patrick, ill. II. Title. III. Series: Holidays and festivals (Compass Point Books)
F1233.F618 2003
394.262–dc21   2002155742

Table of Contents

NOTE: *In this book, words that are defined in the glossary are in* **bold** *the first time they appear in the text.*

Wave the Mexican flag. Dance and sing. Join the parade to celebrate Mexico's freedom and the freedom of all Americans!

Cinco de Mayo (SEEN-co day MA-yo) means "the fifth of May." Cinco de Mayo is a Mexican holiday that falls on that day. It is quickly becoming an American holiday, too. Mexico is a country just south of the United States.

Each year on May 5, Mexicans remember the men and women who fought in the Battle of Puebla in Mexico in 1862. They honor the soldiers who kept the French from taking control of their country. The holiday celebrates freedom and liberty.

In the United States, Mexican Americans (also called Chicanos) celebrate the holiday in a different way. They go to parties, hold parades, and put on plays that show pride in their Mexican heritage. They proudly carry the Mexican flag and perform Mexican songs and dances throughout the day.

The First
People of Mexico

Thousands of years ago, many different groups of people lived in the country now called Mexico. Three of the largest groups were the Maya (MY-ah), the Aztec (AZ-tek), and the Tolteca (tol-TAY-cah). They lived in large cities that contained buildings called **pyramids**. Over time, these groups came to be known as Indians.

The Aztec were the most famous of these Indian groups. They wandered for hundreds of years before they settled down and built cities. A legend says that the Aztec god told the people where to build. He said they should look for an eagle eating a snake on top of a cactus. Once they found the eagle, they were to build a city. When the Aztec found an eagle on an island in a lake, they built the city of Tenochtitlan (tay-NOCH-tee-tlan). It means "Place of the Nopal Cactus." After many years, Tenochtitlan became a very important center for trade and religion. At one time, it was one of the largest cities in the ancient world. Today, this place is called Mexico City.

Living Under Spanish Rule

During the 1500s, soldiers from Spain came to Mexico to look for riches. They took control of the land and made the Indians slaves. The Spaniards ruled for three hundred years. They treated the Indians badly. Many Spaniards married Indian women. Their children were called *mestizos* because they were both Spanish and Indian. Today, most people who live in Mexico are mestizos.

Over time, the Spanish rulers in Mexico borrowed a lot of money from other countries. One of the countries was France. The Mexican government could not pay back the money it borrowed. Therefore, the French government sent an army to take control of Mexico.

The Battle of Puebla
(Batalla de Puebla)

On the morning of May 5, 1862, the French army stopped near the small town of Puebla. The army was on its way to Mexico City. The people of Puebla did not want the French in their country. They attacked them and drove them back. Within a few hours, the French army left. However, it returned a year later. This time, the French took control of Mexico City and set up a new leader. For the next five years, the Mexican people tried to get rid of the French. Mexican leader Benito Juarez led the fight against them.

JUAREZ

A Holiday
of Freedom!

In 1867, the French left Mexico for good. Benito Juarez became president of Mexico and made May 5 a national holiday. Now, every year on May 5, people of Mexican **descent** remember the brave men and women of Puebla. They fought the first battle against the French and won their freedom.

Mexicans are proud of how brave their **ancestors** were in battle. To honor them today, leaders give speeches about bravery. People hold street fairs and parades. There is music, dancing, and every favorite Mexican food you can eat.

Favorite Mexican Foods

Mexicans are known for their special meals. Their dishes are a mix of foods from Mexico and the southwestern parts of the United States. Some of the most popular foods are tamales (ta-MA-lees), enchiladas (en-che-LAH-dahs), tortillas (tor-TEE-yas), tacos (TAH-cos) burritos (buh-REE-tos), frijoles (free-HO-lees), and churros (CHU-ros).

Many Mexican meals include tortillas and frijoles. A tortilla is a thin, flat bread made from wheat flour or corn dough. Frijoles are beans. Enchiladas are rolled-up tortillas filled with beans and chopped meat, chicken, or cheese.

The enchilada may have come from a Mayan dish that rich people ate on special occasions. Enchiladas are topped with sauce and cheese. Today, most of these sauces are called salsas and are made from tomatoes and spices such as garlic and chili peppers.

Tacos are corn or flour tortillas folded over a meat or cheese filling. Burritos are large flour tortillas wrapped around a meat, cheese, and bean filling. Tamales are made of cornmeal dough mixed with chopped pork or chicken. They are put in wet corn **husks** and are steamed. For dessert, many people eat churros, which are long pieces of fried dough covered in sugar and cinnamon.

Favorite
Mexican Music

Mexican music is a rich blend of Indian and Spanish sounds. Before the Spaniards came to Mexico, people played music with rattles, drums, reed or clay flutes, and horns made from shells. When the Spaniards came, they brought violins, guitars, harps, and brass horns.

Mariachi (mar-ee-AH-chee) is one popular type of Mexican music. Mariachi music goes back hundreds of years. At one time, it was known as the music of country people. Today, mariachi bands help celebrate special moments in the lives of Mexican people. You can hear this music at birthdays, weddings, funerals, special holidays, and church festivals. Often, people use the music to send messages of love to one another.

The Mexican
Hat Dance

The Mexican hat dance is called *jarabe tapatio* (hah-RAH-bay tah-pah-TEE-o). It is the main dance of Mexico. Dancers wear special costumes when they perform the dance. Men wear an outfit called a *charro*. This outfit includes a short jacket, tight pants, and boots. The pants and jacket have pretty patterns sewn on them. Women wear a scarf, called a *rebozo*, over their shoulders. They also wear a colorful skirt.

The dance begins when a man tosses his hat or *sombrero* (som-BRAY-ro) on the floor in front of a woman. If she likes the man, she will dance on the wide brim of the hat. Sometimes, the owner of the hat will take quick hopping steps around his own hat.

Celebrating in the United States

In the United States, Chicanos celebrate Cinco de Mayo in a way different from the people of Mexico. In Mexico, people celebrate freedom on this day. They honor those who fought against an army twice their size and won.

In the United States, Chicanos celebrate their heritage. They do things to show pride in their Mexican **culture.** Cinco de Mayo is a popular holiday in the states of Texas and Arizona. A great number of people of Mexican descent live there.

Many Chicano families begin their celebration of Cinco de Mayo by going to church. Then they prepare special meals. Usually, people dress in red, white, and green clothing, which are the colors of the Mexican flag. They have parties with Mexican songs and dances. At neighborhood stores, people can buy Mexican food, music, clothing, books, and toys. At schools, children can go to special events to honor their culture.

Today, more and more schools throughout the United States are adding Cinco de Mayo to their holiday calendars. They are making this holiday another way to celebrate the freedom and liberty of everyone.

Things You Might
See on Cinco de Mayo

The Mexican Flag

Three large stripes make up the Mexican flag. The green stripe stands for freedom from Spanish rule. The white stands for freedom of religion. The red stands for unity, or teamwork. In the center of the flag is an eagle with a snake in its mouth. This picture is the Mexican coat of arms. It is based on a legend that says the Aztecs built a city on the spot where they saw an eagle eating a snake on top of a cactus. Today, this city is called Mexico City.

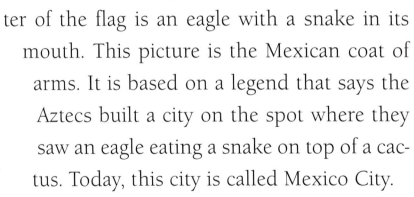

24

Sombreros

A sombrero is a tall hat with a wide brim. The word sombrero comes from the Spanish word *sombra,* which means "shade." There are two kinds of sombreros. One is made from straw. The other is made from felt and has designs sewn on it. Usually, tiny wooden balls or beads hang from the brim of the hat.

The first people to wear sombreros may have been mestizo workers in Mexico or Texas. As they worked, they needed a hat to keep the hot sun out of their face and eyes. Today, the sombrero is used mainly in the Mexican hat dance.

Serapes

A *serape* (sa-RAH-pay) is a cape worn over the shoulders. In Mexico, usually only men wear a serape. The serape looks like a rug with a hole cut in the middle for a head to fit through. During Cinco de Mayo celebrations, men often wear a serape and a sombrero.

A Mariachi Band

A mariachi band has three to twelve people in it. The musicians play violins, trumpets, guitars, and bass instruments. They sing favorite country songs called **folk songs**. "La Cucaracha" (lah coo-ca-RAH-cha) is a popular folk song. It means "the cockroach" in Spanish.

Mariachi musicians dress in colorful costumes. They often wear sombreros. Some people think that mariachi bands got their start when the French army ruled Mexico. Many French soldiers married Mexican women and hired small bands to play at their weddings. The bands were later called mariachi, which sounds like the French word for wedding, *mariage* (mah-ree-AHJ).

A Piñata

Children have fun breaking open a *piñata* (pen-YAH-tah) at parties. A piñata is made of cardboard and **papier-mâché**. Usually, it is shaped like an animal or a star. The piñata is filled with candy and toys and is hung from the ceiling. Children cover their eyes with a piece of cloth. Then they take turns trying to hit the piñata with a stick. When it breaks open, everyone scrambles to get the gifts that fall to the ground.

What You Can Do on Cinco de Mayo

Over the years, Cinco de Mayo has become a holiday filled with song, dance, and tasty foods. On this day, however, it is also important to honor the men and women who gave their lives so that others could be free. Cinco de Mayo celebrates liberty and freedom, which are important to everyone. Here are some things you can do on the fifth of May.

* Celebrate your freedom by helping others!
* Go out of your way to help someone solve a problem.
* Show a family member or friend how to settle differences without fighting.
* Make your own book about Cinco de Mayo.
* Plan a Cinco de Mayo party at your home or school.

Glossary

ancestors a person's grandparents, great-grandparents, and so on

celebrates has a party or honors a special event

culture a group of people's beliefs, customs, and way of life

descent the family a person comes from

folk songs songs handed down from one generation to the next

heritage beliefs and customs that are important to a certain group of people and that are handed down from one generation to the next

husks the dry coverings of certain fruits and seeds

national holiday a holiday that is celebrated by the entire country and that usually includes a day off from work or school

papier-mâché paper pulp with glue that makes a light material used for shaping and molding things

pyramids solid buildings with sloping sides that come together at the top

Where You Can Learn More about Cinco de Mayo

At the Library

Bradley, Mignon L., and Carrie Huber. *Cinco de Mayo: An Historical Play.* Santa Barbara, Calif.: Luisa Productions, 1981.

Garcia, James. *Cinco de Mayo: A Mexican Holiday of Unity and Pride.* Chanhassen, Minn.: The Child's World, 2002.

Urrutia, Maria Cristina, and Rebeca Orozco. *Cinco de Mayo: Yesterday and Today.* Toronto, Ont.: Groundwood Books, 2002.

On the Web

Kiddyhouse: Cinco de Mayo
http://www.kiddyhouse.com/Holidays/Cinco/
To read a history of the holiday and to learn arts and crafts related to Cinco de Mayo

Kids Domain: Holidays
http://www.kidsdomain.com/holiday/cinco/crafts.html
To learn how to make crafts for Cinco de Mayo

Through the Mail

The Center for Mexican American Studies
West Mall Building
Suite 5.102, MC F9200
The University of Texas at Austin
Austin, TX 78712
For information about the Latino experience and ongoing educational projects

On the Road

The Mexican Museum
Fort Mason Center, Building D
San Francisco, CA 94123
415/202-9700
To view Latino art and to learn about the link between Mexico and the Americas

Lo Nuestro Cinco de Mayo Festival
1901 Bergman Ave
Austin, TX 78702
512/867-1999
To celebrate Hispanic heritage with music, food, art, games, and more

Index

About the Author and Illustrator

Alice K. Flanagan writes books for children and teachers. Since she was a young girl, she has enjoyed writing. She has written more than seventy books. Some of her books include biographies of U.S. presidents and their wives, biographies of people working in our neighborhoods, phonics books for beginning readers, and informational books about birds and Native Americans. Alice K. Flanagan lives in Chicago, Illinois.

Patrick Girouard has been drawing and painting for many years. He has illustrated more than fifty books for children. Patrick has two sons, Marc and Max, and a dog called Sam. They all live in Indiana.